Rapture in Arrears

Erotic poetry by
S.A. Harper

Word Oyster Press

For other work published by
Word Oyster Press
please visit
wordoyster.com

You may contact the writer at:
saharper@wordoyster.com

There are no content and/or trigger warnings.
It's poetry. You can handle it.

ISBN-13: 978-0-9977084-4-8

Other work by S.A. Harper

Poetry

All These Pronouns Jump Bones

Short Stories

Feeding the Two-Backed Beast
Ephemeral
Tweed

Contents

"Free verse really got rolling about a hundred years ago. It wasn't just free in the sense of being very loose in the rhyme and meter department. Free verse was sexually free. That's what nobody understands. Free verse meant free, naked, unclothed, un-Victorian people scampering about in an unfettered sort of way. That's why it was so exciting."

— Nicholson Baker, *The Anthologist*

Bladderwrack

It's too hot for anything else.
We eat Popsicles in facing beach chairs,
one foot between each other's legs.
Gulls shriek. Wind blows. Toes wiggle.

Later, I trace your edges in the sand,
leave the beach to pee, return to find
your body still there, sparkling in sunlight,
reaching up for me from within the lines.

The tide comes in. Your outline washes away.
I brush the sand off your shoulders, lay you back down
on a towel my parents bought in Clearwater,
kneel, bend, and pull your suit aside.

It's not so much the heart of the matter as the crux.
Not so much the crux as the center.
Not so much the center as the target.
Not so much the target as the focus.
Not so much the focus as the bean.
The bean. The bean. The flickable lickable bean.

The taste of you is lost in sea salt.
But here are the usual fingers in my hair,
your well-known pulse, your sunset heat,
your Irish moss, your dune, your cove.

We've stayed too long. We have places to be.

Washing the Sex Toys

The top rack is full of borosilicate glass —
plugs and bulbs and knobby wands,
the double-ended one curving back
to point one way twice (adjacent objectives),
its surface purple as supermarket eggplant.
The "Sanitize" setting strikes me as judgy.

There's a spray for the silicone and plastic —
the stock-still dildos, the jittery vibrators,
all the clamps, hooks, paddles, rings, and beads.
The spray has a new-car fragrance.
Cleaned toys smell more of their origin than of us,
more of the factory than happy circumstance.

I sort the colored ropes, wrap them in coils,
allow them the company of harnesses and straps.
With everything laid out all clean on the bed,
the display impresses with its audacity —
so much for so little, all this for just us two,
buying trinkets for our accessorized pleasure.

You-calyptus

I am not entirely without environmental concern.
I am aware of the world beyond your undressing,
how this is the earliest I've ever seen you in shorts.

You distract me with tales of belching cows while
I imagine how I can see the ozone hole beckoning
from the middle of your Southern Hemisphere.

I can care about Australian sun and your cooter,
metaphorically able to picket and finger you
at the same time. I'm dedicated like that.

I won't stop until you cry like a koala.
I won't stop until the echidnas sue for peace.
I won't stop until we scare off the rising tide.

Nostalgia Never Was What It Used to Be

She yells up from the living room
the way she's always done. I flinch. Same.
Of course, now that she's in her 80s,
she's less likely to start up the stairs
the way she did when I was a teen,
and she'd beat on my door with her fists.

I wanted to show you my room.
No one's lived up here since I moved out.
More attic than bedroom, it's stifling hot
with a slanted ceiling too short for an adult.
That wall there had blacklight posters.
This wall had Raquel Welch wearing skins.

You're kneeling on the very spot where
Bobby spilled Testors model lacquer
and melted the shine off three floor tiles.
The shape still reminds me of South America.
Your mouth is warmer than Medellin.
My mother talks, but we refuse to hear.

This never happened to me in this room.
For years, I got off by myself in this bed.
Now it's covered with junk for a flea market
my mother stopped selling at five years
before the venue closed in a sales tax scandal.
I was never a sock or lotion guy.

The family cat died in that corner
without warning one Thanksgiving morning.
I nudged her with my foot, but I already knew.
I probably shouldn’t be able to come at all
with my mother’s voice still resonating, unzipped
before a ghost cat’s translucent disdain.

But I do.
You’re just that good.

Haiku I

You ask to be spanked.
For a second date, this is —
hands down — my best yet.

~

cozy in your arms,
this afterglow is ideal
‘cept for the puddle

~

April overflows.
We hear the gutters cascade.
Your mouth spills my seed.

~

my legs sometimes cramp
when I take her from behind
the show must go on

I’ve tried to forget
the feel, the heft of her breasts.
But my hands? Just so.

~

sorry if I jumped
but one prefers tongue to teeth
in the thick of things

~

Old sheets on the bed?
Secret birthday plans for you
might soon get messy.

~

berries smashed on skin
prudent summer lovers know
save a quart for pie

Pinned

Your willing wrists are made for seizing:
the right size for ten fingers encircling,
the proper someone's firm hold tightening,
the half-circle grip of his hands closing,
the look in his eyes effectively silencing
what's left of your half-forgotten struggle.

Consent asked and already given, today you find
you're made to have the weight of his body
pushed like columns down to solid pediment,
and you pressed into feathers and thread count,
the hissing surrender of air from a pillow,
your eyes first wide, then falling closed,

your breathless lips briefly bitten shut,
too sealed to say halt to him or anyone,
fingers reaching and clawing at air,
clutching up at cherubs circling,
nude their wings approving,
your hands pierced again,

your lips bitten again,
wounds recurring
as you are at last
nailed to the bed —
a butterfly,
pinned.

Entrance / Entracte

One inserts. One engulfs.
One envelops as the other invades.
Penetration salsas with consumption,
opening doors, rushing through doors,
pushing against door jambs
only to find the door jambs pushing back.

This is how the beast is made.
This is where we find our fervent angels.

Rode Hard, Ordered Pizza

Distance-muffled frat boys howl horny in late-night fog
as he and I stop mid-Quad, shooting rock-paper-scissors
to pick the room our 'nads need, pronto.
Tie. Tie. Rock wins. His.

I kissed him at the bar, and he passed muster,
the best this fall and it's almost Halloween.
His eagerness improves on his bed as comfort
equals confidence. Buttons open, one by one.

Two Long Island Iced Teas past discretion,
there's no false freshman modesty as I undress.
I own tonight's every anticipated decision, even this
dorm-room, stinky-socks, fairy-lights rendezvous.

I'm first to throw a leg, so I'm on top. No guts, no glory.
I silently praise his unlofted bed and grind away,
up on my arms enough for him to knead my boobs
like a newly-opened pack of Model Magic.

Forward and back, I drag my pussy along his cock
as if I'm slathering warm butter on toast. Fair play,
he grabs my butt and rips it apart like challah.
I bite his nipple just because I'm starved.

He wants in more than he wants good grades,
excellent weed, or his father's stubborn approval.
I make him wait until he twitches, make him moan
before I dare the dismount and reverse,

a move I imagined more graceful in my head,
cowgirl retaking the saddle, pommel style.
Slipping him inside, there's no resistance.
No rodeo clowns required. The crowd goes wild.

He thrusts away inside me as if it's a gallop
when what I'm wanting is more canter or trot.
The anime girl on his wall flashes me a peace sign,
so I play tortoise to his hare until he tuckers out.

Leaning forward on his shins, sharp as a table's edge,
I can't bring myself to care what he can or cannot see:
the hair I missed shaving, the skin I refuse to bleach,
the crinkled hole he thumbs like he's riffling a book.

None of that matters as I slowly rise and fall,
grabbing on the upstroke, engulfing on the drop,
building speed, knowing it's a race to the finish.
Anime girl sees me touching myself and winks.

The condom's in a Kleenex in a trashcan 'cross the room.
I let him lick my boobs to reward his good aim.
The dorm's alive with DoorDash smells of food
not meant for us. Famished, I hand him his phone.

In Defense of Shortcake

You judge me for my flecks of bean,
most flavorful of the easy weekend lays,
tongue-kiss missionary, set of sticky spoons.

Only someone who regularly bakes
knows how a good cook adds vanilla
to all the tasty things.

Tucking In

Our three-year-old's
    best friend's
    mother
        has a red carnation tattoo
        on her left ass cheek.
That may seem an odd detail for me to know
except — this morning — it's not even half.

Our three-year-old
    and her best friend
    had a sleepover last night,
        and my wife and I
        were invited to sleep over, too.
But my wife and I weren't asked by
one child or both, but instead by
our three-year-old's
    best friend's
    mother, Joanie
        (who also has a C-section scar
        and surprising flexibility).
My wife tells me in the pantry that Jerry
was an enthusiastic lover but dull.

Our three-year-old
    and her best friend
    have two bowls of Froot Loops each
        while the four of us blush
        our way through eggs and toast —
grinning at our children,
avoiding each other's eyes.

Lateral Move

Can't say I didn't see it coming —
my muse turning up on OnlyFans.
Gotta be more fulfilling flashing her tiddies for tips
than trying to inspire a poet whose nouns, adverbs,
keyboard, Number 2 pencils are all missing, no action.

After all, even a muse has student loans to pay,
and there were only going to be so many waking hours
a woman could waste whispering in my ear
before ultimately starting to resent
how I never write anything down.

It's quiet now.
It's quiet now.

The voice-no-longer-in-my-head has a Sybian
that writes sonnets with 21 speeds and random patterns.
Weeknights, she can be found on Chaturbate,
didactically rubbing them out in free verse,
wearing white cat ears, wearing red fox tails.

She takes nude selfies in bar bathroom mirrors
after scrawling dirty haiku in every other stall.
On occasion, she inscribes her best words on ice
and devours them with her other mouth.
I understand she's writing a book.

I can hear myself think.
Why would I want to hear myself think?

I’m aware she’s living her best life
while I sit here spinning 16-plus wheels
connected to no axles, no cart,
no horse of this or any other color.
I wonder if she misses me.

I’ve left a new notebook in the window.
She knows she can use my best pen.

Haiku II

such a good kisser
might do well to hide his light
beneath my bushel

~

if you float my boat
I'll paddle until you come
to find a wet spot

~

Screw what the heart wants!
There are times one must accept
what the pussy needs.

~

We stop. A reprieve.
I delay your little death;
then we start again.

what I have in mind
won't take all of your fingers
one — or two — will do

~

body paint was fun
until we read the fine print
purple nipples suck

~

After all, what is
a little blood between friends?
Put down a towel.

~

Bastard stirs his tea.
I sit tied, vibrating toy:
no release, no scone.

As Lockdown Lingers, June 2020

We've grown closer in this faux quarantine —
closer but less appropriate over time, as it
settles in, drags on, all our filters falling away,

our bodies separate and bare in harsh spring light,
perhaps wearing half or likely not wearing at all
yesterday's informal wrinkled clothes,

me no longer adjusting the camera
to hide the random blemish,
you not bothering to hide the tampon string
I would never see if you were here.

We fix dinner, eat our meals on Skype.
I discuss my friends. You read your mail.
We play games online until bedtime.

Night after night, we watch each other come.
We watch each other watch each other come.

This is the ouroboros COVID makes of us —
you end where I begin, head to tail,
miles apart, resolution limited,
daily done, somehow unresolved.

Forsythia

The month separating
    cabin fever
        from
    spring fever
it is a transition without markers —
a membrane, a scrim, a veil
that no longer keeps us in,
no longer keeps us apart,
no longer hides
    the twitching sprout,
    the swollen buds,
    the ring of flowers
pierced at April's insistence.
The days open into sunlight.
The hours spin out until it's dark.

I want no more of spring
    without your taste.
I need no more exposition
    without declaration.

And so we come inside.
We stay inside. We push inside.
Cabin in a cabin,
    at last the fever breaks.

Smart Thermostat

We shelter in conditioned air.
Where once our parents took to movies,
we stay at home, windows closed,
watching the leaves outside rustle
in an imagined torrid breeze.

Clothing is reduced to its essence.
I've worn only boxers for days.
You pad around in a tank top
and a parade of patterned panties,
both boy short and briefs. Simple. Cool.

Last night, we snuck onto the deck,
and beneath a waning gibbous moon
I fucked you fast against the railing.
Not enough water for mosquitoes,
we lingered after and fingered

still humming bits at arm's length,
thinking of colder weather and goosebumps,
of tightened skin, balls held close,
of cries unable to exit windows
shut fast to hold in our heat.

How much longer does this persist?
How long until all puddles merge?

Candle, Lit Three Ways

Taken from your drawer,
I've stuffed you up good:
plain white in your bum,
purple stripes in your pussy,
and red lace in your mouth,
each with bits still sticking out,
little panty wicks set to light
or — failing fire — to pull.

Methuselah's Walking Stick

The old cock
plays a waiting game.
He cheats at checkers.
He prolongs Monopoly.
He bets a losing hand
and folds when the chips are down.

The old cock
has time to consider
the derivation of "todger."

The old cock
remembers eight coeds' touch,
the many fingers with their guiding grips
and their roving brush of chaos.
He recalls the smell taste tightness
of nine ports in a storm.

The old cock
thinks back to when he could still
hold up a wet washrag.

The old cock
is slow to the party
and often leaves early.
He likes to tell long stories
but now and then forgets the point.
He lets the knees pull focus.

The old cock
doesn't even bother getting hard in dreams
because he's seen how all that ends.

The old cock
sniffs up all the wrong alleys.
He knows one pill makes you larger
and that brevity isn't always the soul of wit.
He's grown used to second billing,
following close on the heels of a tongue
or an index finger crooked just so.

The old cock
wakes up in the morning
with other things on his mind.

Haiku III

What's stiff is useful:
prick, finger, tongue sinking deep.
Most pots need stirring.

~

breasts are more fun than
a barrel full of monkeys
and far less noisy

~

Your Mom's sweater rack?
In your room, transformed.
Last night's spreader bar!

~

The first buds of May
become flowers for plucking.
Even they want that.

Sitting on my chest,
she faces away, content
with the task at hand.

~

July goldfinches
all wish they were red-tailed hawks.
Me, just eight inches.

~

an “alien probe” —
the crackpots’ way of saying
they enjoy butt stuff.

~

slow our summer sex
languorous lazy fingers
dandle absently

Drifting (A Walk with Jackie)

This is what long winters do to us all.
I barely know you, but you call me anyway,
inviting yourself over in the middle of a storm:
six inches on the ground, another five to fall.

Campus to off-campus, you're eight minutes away.
"It's so quiet right now. No one's out. Let's walk."
You don't take off your coat. I brush the snow off
your hat, pull the door shut, and we set off in the dark.

Ours are the only footprints on unshoveled sidewalks.
We could walk in the street; there are no cars or plows.
And you were right. There's no sound but us,
plodding along, talking about nothing, hands in pockets.

Halfway around the loop, a squad car appears, pulls up,
calls us over. Less suspicious than foolish, the cop tells us
to go home. Two miles, one hour away from my place,
it's not like we have a better choice. We walk on.

I light the second gas stove in my one-room apartment,
and we spread our coats out to dry. Past midnight,
we drink hot chocolate at the table. Quiet now,
you make no move to go. "Stay here, if you want."

You say you'll sleep in the chair. I get you an afghan,
turn out the lights, take off my clothes, get into bed.
"Would you rather get in here with me?" You don't say yes.
But you slip under my blankets and sheet, fully clothed.

Another inch of snow falls, and we exchange 47 kisses
before you start to throw out clothes, both of us careful
to keep our underwear on because everyone knows
underwear is the best form of contraception.

On your hands and knees, you teach me the meaning
of *frottage*, grinding on my boner through all that cotton,
you so close to coming even before I reach my hand around
to find what's making your panties damp, edging in.

I feel you've done this part before. Wary from the start,
you stroke me from above, palm over the head
like putting an umbrella on a geyser. No tourists sprayed.
I get you a tissue. A plow goes by. We cuddle. We sleep.

In two years, I'll learn you've rented this same apartment.
By then, I'll have forgotten what you told me that night.
You'll forget why you made the call, why we took the walk.
People meet. They join. They drift away like snow.

California King

Tracing circles on your back, I ponder
the stories that skin tells skin
    in the night when we touch,
    at dawn when we touch,
    on long afternoons like these
        when we lay splayed
        on sweat-ruined beds,
        dripping from our desires,
        meeting in our middles,
        rotated off-kilter
        like crosses formed from our own beams,
    touching just enough for our flushed skins
    to whisper highlights of their secrets.

Sometimes our skins talk of scars.
Sometimes they speak in superlatives
    of things they've learned from other skins:
        the best feathery caress,
        the worst careless clasp,
        one man's frantic thrashing against,
        another woman's gentle lingering clutch.

Sometimes they complain of bras.

Our skins tell these stories —
    each pore, each freckle, each hair
    chatty in recollection, their collective memory
    of pleasure and pain like singing songs —
together, they are both chorus and cacophony,
assuming we hear, hoping we'll listen.

Bottomless

My lips cover my teeth like fine slipcovers,
my epiglottis chill as Bad Bunny at Coachella.
I practiced ten nights running, two fingers fathoming
my mouth, bright blue dildo suction-cupped to a mirror,
eyes crossing, nose advancing, glasses retreating,

trying to imagine your balls tip-tapping my chin,
my nose in your scruffy hair, and between those two
my tongue allowing you to pass without catching,
without choking, all the while thinking how much better
skin and blood and spunk would eventually be.

Why'd I master this skill if I'm not going to have you
halfway down my throat by now on a night like this,
my mother on her way back to Chillicothe
having stacked my magazines, judged my clothes,
checked my bathroom for your imagined toothbrush,

peeked in my bedside table at my condoms, my cuffs,
any sign that I'm half the woman her sisters fear I am?
My hair's in pigtails, handles set for the skull fucking
I'll consent to when you show up, fluffed in the foyer,
unzipped at the door, finally ready for consumption.

Kudzu

in through a window
once thought closed,
around my ankle
a single tendril wraps.
under blankets
tucked in tight,
glowing green
in midnight black,
from dirt's decay
to clean white sheets,
from soil's promise
to fresh-washed skin,
a second vine, the other ankle,
not holding me down until…
not pulling me apart until…
not prying me open until
ten, no twenty,
a hundred
other tendrils
join.

Watch How We Play

We split one of my father's beers
and played Hungry Hungry Hippos,
fingers buttery from popcorn,
flailing pounding laughing
as all the marbles flew.

Soon I found a way
to sucker you into wrestling me
half-clothed, half-sober
because so much I wanted you
to pin me on my parent's couch.

Later, I would mistakenly swear
I came for the very first time
as you gobbled my breasts like a hippo,
me mistaking conscious contractions
for an unstoppable rollercoaster plummet.

Only now I know what it was like
to not really know anything at all:
dry humping to Tommy James,
riding your bulge until I throbbed,
wishing they'd never come home.

Haiku IV

his open book falls
the air conditioner drips
hard he dreams of you

~

Fingered in the woods,
your cries echo tree to tree,
making possums smile.

~

shower me with cum
squirt like a summer sprinkler
all our droughts must end

~

She's looking at porn,
thinking of someone she knows,
when the cat walks in.

You, me, an ice cube:
in whose open mouth it's in
when the other melts.

~

Her ass and her tits:
original equipment.
Older, still the same.

~

there is no bad mood
that cannot be made better
by a well-placed tongue

~

Early September:
bugs whir outside as if to
mock your Rabbit's hum.

Brat

It's easy to see which way this goes —
who is the spoiled, who's the one who spoils?
I always push you to this limit
because I know you'll break.
And then I'm over your knee
like a damp bath sheet,
    a rolled-up carpet,
    a pillow heavy with mites,
    a cat uninterested in levitation,
    a ball of clay waiting to be shaped,
struggling against my cravings,
your hold, your hands,
the warming slaps
and stinging blows,
my small desire for you to stop
    quickly overridden
    by my sizable need
    for you to continue.
Tomorrow I might behave.
But where's the fun in that?

Waiting Game

Ankle to bar to ankle,
one wrist to another and back to bar,
I sacrifice modesty and comfort for purpose,
ass tipped in the air, face down, flush on the floor.
Bottoms up, as it were. No holes barred.

I await the unseen expected:
their fingers, tongue, lubed-up prick,
vibrator, dildo, thick steel plug,
the clothespins and string to tug apart,
the cold steel hook to hoist aloft.

My muscles strain, extended full.
In this position not meant for holding,
my energy is expended in waiting.
This is the shudder that comes before the shiver.
A door closes. I smile as footsteps approach.

Stag, Vixen, Chair (and Tyler from Walmart)

Six dining table chairs and — somehow —
we've chosen the squeakiest one.

It's you, sitting on me, sitting on a chair
that constantly creaks as if it tolerates but objects
to finding itself in our den without its sibling chairs,
just our three bare butts — an unlikely occurrence
in the life of a chair before now. So, the chair abides as

I hold you naked on my lap, your legs outside mine,
your bony back, your shoulders against my chest,
your ass pressing my afterthought into my stomach,
my nose tickled by the hair behind your neck,
my left hand between your thighs, unsurprised

that we've barely begun, and you're so-soon-sopping
at the novel notion — two pricks all for you.

I have three fingers folded around your throat,
my forefinger and thumb pressed against your cheek
so I can feel what you feel, this other man's cock
slip-sliding away inside your drooling face.
He is tall but stands on a stool. He towers above

our heads, these lips of yours I kissed before he arrived,
this mouth of yours I will take myself before he leaves.

Equilibrium punctured, your breathing evolves.
I hear your moans bubble up like cooking oats,
how twice you almost choke on the spoon.
He holds your head stock-still, hair pulled,
his fingers so close it makes my eyes cross.

I cannot see around you, cannot know whether
you're pinching your breasts or rolling his balls.

You wriggle. The chair creaks.
He thrusts. The chair creaks.
One of your hands presses my hand, insinuates
two fingers inside you. I curl them and coax
until you quiver. The chair creaks.

All this time, my erection has been unwitnessed.
I feel it leaking between us — my stomach, your spine —

the one thing the chair doesn't see.
If the chair could talk, perhaps tomorrow
it would tell its friends what made it blush,
describe in detail what it was like to be a chair
watching me watch him fuck you.

Inheritance

This is how life carries on.
This is how spirits are made.

On the night she's buried,
we have sex in my mother's house,
in Aunt Lou's four-poster bed,
beneath a tattered homemade quilt,
        in front of the silhouettes
                of three Revolutionary women
                whose names are all Mary.
I come in your ass
and not one ghost says a word.

The bedsprings squeak ad infinitum.
The bedsprings squeak like a dirge.

Petting Without a License

Clandestine turgid treasures
fast uncovered with unsnapped ease,
revealed by rasping zippers' descent,
as we reach in,
          take out,
            pull aside,
              slip between.

We claim what we find as ours,
these monsters of blood and promise,
these toys of passion and convenience.

What's yours is mine, mine yours.
We stroke their fur until they're tame.

Bashful Blather

In the bar, someone's cued up "Psycho Killer."
Its heartbeat bassline carries down the hall
to the Men's where I'm confronting hands-on
a cock conundrum: a bladder made bashful
by a voyeur's desire to glance behind and gawk.

I lock eyes with the urinal cake, neither of us
certain how I'll ever be able to pee
when not far behind my back these two
are going at it full-tilt, pants down, bits out,
fucking in a doorless bathroom stall.

"Fa fa fa fa fa fa fa fa fa..." Run away?
But three beers down, I very much need to go.
We're in audio porn territory, belts hitting tile,
their moans and such making me hard —
not something conducive to flow.

"I hate people when they're not polite."
I could take my predicament to the other stall,
but that's even closer to their groans and squeals.
I close my eyes, trying to imagine I'm listening
to a podcast I might want to subscribe to later.

I hold on, determined to wait them out,
worried they're waiting for me to leave,
our standoff joint and sublime. Disrupted?
"Hey! You wanna come give us a hand?"
Hardly hanging, they had me at hello.

Vampire, Invited In

The tissue that separates
her request from her permission
is transparent in its execution
and thinnest in its logic.

It rends before the first tear falls.
It shreds before ropes tighten into knots,
before I entertain what's possible
with all we have to work with:

handcuffs, cord, black cloth gag,
a wicked wheel with pointy spikes,
a feather to tickle, a slapper to sting.

Her shocked hesitation is disingenuous,
as if all this isn't shown only by appointment.
Nothing manifests of its own volition.
This is less entreaty than behest.

In her bedroom, there is a box.
Five minutes ago, she gave me the key.

Haiku V

a thorough mess made
melted Halloween candy
my mouth your fanny

~

flat my tongue lies still
when your thighs' trembling stops
then I'll start again

~

Hang up your halo.
I'm not here to worship you,
even though I kneel.

~

Finish what you start.
The girl you leave half-eaten
remembers the slight.

I belong in you
like Nilla Wafers in a
banana pudding.

~

Admit your limits.
They'll know before you do
if it's a threesome.

~

In these, I fail you:
can't talk dirty, barely dance.
My fingers redeem.

~

she sees me watching
might not be an accident
how her towel falls

It Should Bother Me More I Did the Math

In this room, there is a ceiling
made of 238 unremarkable acoustic tiles,
each with exactly 484 nondescript holes.
This comes to 115,192 holes above my bed,

none of which can be connected to form her face.
A pillow is nothing like her arm.
Her skin didn't resemble a wall at all,
and grapefruit are always citrus, nothing more.

If there's anything holes know,
it's an absence, the certainty of a void.
Holes know the volume of what's not there.
They know what's missing, the sum of all holes.

I can't seem to make something from anything,
can't cajole overlooked love notes from pockets,
can't conjure a rabbit from a wistful sow's ear.
And even sure signs of her — the empty

dresser drawers, a desiccated bar of Dove —
I try to add them all together, mix and match,
and can't quite construct a smile, a wink,
a shared sandwich, a stolen Cheez-It,

one whiskey kiss followed by another,
two stout legs opening wide in longing ache,
the three times she said maybe before yes,
turned over and got up on her knees,

offering me the dealer's choice for free,
this or that, details of which are forgotten,
lost in these uncharted constellations
with no fortunes or possible greater meaning.

The holes above my head should spell it out,
draw a picture, dot-to-dot, make it clear how she
(user of that soap, filler of those empty drawers),
has passed on like sleep, faded like 5 a.m. dreams.

These holes should show their calculations,
how she's gone and gone and gone again, all zeros,
how there's no mathematical trick — all holes counted—
that brings her back to this continuing tally,

this unsolved equation,
this space making space for a space.

Saint Uvula of Pomona

In duality, she is both if she is one —
bee-stung lips turned gaping gullet,
purity of this morning's passing peck
now submerged in hoarse sounds hungry,
choking herself with bits of this other,
her mouth and throat replete when filled,
grasping his ass and heaving him close
when he neglects to push inside this far,
forgetting to think in terms of absolution,
briefly unmindful of her need to breathe,
in the end, only conscious of a time
to swallow, a time to take the weight off
and rise from love-made-tender knees.

Explanation ≠ Vindication

As far as
the perineum goes,
hers is shorter than mine.
Thus my surprise
when drunkly pressing
in our queen-sized dusk
I popped myself
into a wee surprise.
It's fair to say
aspersions
were
cast.

Nosh

Let me be the cantaloupe
in your edible arrangement.
Line me up with willing others —
the strawberries, the pineapple.

Make simple chairs our skewers
and place us naked in an untidy arc.
With all our limbs excited apart
(sitting forward, leaning back,
contemplating tongues and Fruit Fresh),
crawl before us blindfolded,
not knowing each from each,
and sniff us all unseeing,
or taste us, vine to flesh to tree.

I am the sweetness you desire,
the smell your gut can't forget,
the lips on your lips you remember.
If you find me, I am yours.

And, unlike the honeydew, I'll be ripe.

Spanked in a Meadow

cool breeze
bare bottom

braced eager
startled still

slaps sting
birds fly

warmth spreads
pain and pain and pain

pink prickles
blotches bloom

redeeming rub
goosebump chill

the finger
the finger
the finger

Proof through the Night

Three towns over, the distant fireworks crack,
patchy like the last kernels in a microwave,
erratic until the all-at-once, garbage time finale.
The pyrotechnicians are taking nothing home tonight.

We could have gone and watched, but didn't.
We could still turn on the Boston Pops but don't.
We sit on our patio in the dark, watching fireflies,
eating watermelon in our underwear.

I love this more than the flag —
how your ass wiggles as
I pull your bikini briefs down,
how you bend and spread open
for my underlit examination,
how eager you are to take in
whatever comes along to poke.

If we debauched celebrate apart,
if we depraved invent our own show,
these will not be the things per se
that shake our country to its knees.

Playtime

The more kids you have,
the harder it becomes
to get them all sleepovers
                    elsewhere
                    and on the same night
so that you can miss the little darlings
while using adequate birth control
and just-bought hogtie cuffs.

Haiku VI

Flash across the room:
no one else will see but you.
I shaved. Made you look.

~

inadvertent touch
abstinence has its limits
cracks in twilight ice

~

Stale costume drama
made better by popcorn and
your hand in my pants.

~

panties ripped apart
a material witness
might say “asunder”

a chastity belt
with a broken lock is just
metal underwear

~

Perhaps pineapple?
Give him whatever it takes
to sweeten the deal.

~

What else to call it —
the finger that pokes the anus?
Digital asset.

~

this dance ends tonight
what anticipation builds
one touch can finish

herring

she shivers in reverie —
    not ready to sleep,
    unable to rise,
lost in post-coital warmth
    that even now needs no blanket,
amazed by the act of breathing,
        the renewed stillness of air,
        the beating of his nearby heart.

in repetition, she has learned
    the buttons to push —
things that make him take notice,
        that make him gasp and squirm,
        that make him shift stiff in his seat.

youth is an urge best unfiltered,
    temptations surfacing like whales
    blowing spouts of desire on distant horizons.
she's adrift, swimming in seas of that promise —
        the endless shimmer of her silver schools,
        his cock breaking the waves to feed.

respecting the natural order

what rain makes wet,
what desire makes damp,
what seeds make sprout
    with stalks that shoot up
    to stiffen in the sun?

what bulbs burst,
what petals open,
what nectar tempts
    the needle beak to enter
    and with buzzing hover sip?

we are brilliant green spring kisses.
we are sweaty acts of summer passion
and languid nights of autumn afterglow.

what winter threatens, we ignore, willing
to die on this hill, covered in cum.

Knitting Is for Suckers

Routines still new, no new-formed ruts:
working in adjacent rooms, redeemed online,
solitary weekday hours near but apart,
ultimately reunited in nightly leisure:
their takeout dinners with Xbox,
Netflix in socks, shorts or sweats,
time to kill before bedtime,
rinse fuck alarm repeat.

Food Wars holds his interest,
but she's soon distracted,
and begins to play with what's at hand,
rapt at how his ball sack moves:
pulled out, it crawls back in
like an octopus free of its tank —
unpredictable and fluid,
changing shape for changing's sake.

His dick's a more familiar critter.
She knows the touch of her pinky
can make it sit up or flinch;
limp, it still knows party tricks.
It doesn't wait for her attention
before bothering to partly rise.
She watches it settle and twitch,
lost in dreams of what might be.

For one whole episode,
she asks it up, ignores it down
before he asks the top of her head
if maybe he should hit Pause.
She doesn't say yes or no.
She takes the remote,
puts his free hand in her pants,
and chooses an entirely different show.

Dewey Decimal

I recall when I courted chaos
and nothing was by the books
except perhaps that spring semester
making out in the fourth-floor stacks,
shelves pressing in, claustrophobic
cologne and musty paper smell,
me muffled, biting Ben's shoulder
at the sound of approaching voices,
Ben's penis pressed between us,
pointed up and saying hush,
his fingers fixed where they were
beneath my heather tartan skirt,
wet and marking my page.

Not as Flexible (or Absorbent) as I Thought

Shapeless —
    how love bends
        to the ground
    bracing
        for galvanic contact
        hip grab entry thrust —
I bounce.

Indistinct —
    my toes bob
        before my eyes
    fingertips meet floor
        trying to steady knees
        that wobble falter fail —
I bend.

Fluid —
    walking after
        implies motion in space
    time to travel
        across the room
        to choose towel or tissue —
I drip.

Appreciate the Graceful Exit

You call the shots. I'm literally in your hand.
Press, then push. Stretch and pop.
Facing my feet, you sink and settle.
From here, the illusion is complete.
Legerdemain by lube and LED,
I've vanished between your cheeks.

I think of sword swallowers,
how preparation precludes peristalsis.
You squeeze on purpose, not process.
I flex, my response expanding.
Together we indirectly prove
that — unseen — I still exist inside.
You can't enclose what isn't there,
cat neither alive nor dead.

You slowly rock forward and back,
still no sign of reemergence,
no partial reappearance,
just the insistent tug of time,
your fingers that on the far side shake,
slip in and tap on the wall between:

"Hello in there!
Are you well?
Are you fine?"

Traditional, Modern

We learn from experience
that our anniversaries
should always be two-day affairs.

There's one night for overindulging
in wine, memories, conversation,
and servers bringing a multicourse meal.

And then there's a second night
when we stay barefoot at home
and eat much lighter fare.

Our less-encumbered Day Two stomachs
won't interrupt or grumble or complain,
won't object to being jostled or bounced,
won't otherwise make uncomfortable
our planned for and anticipated
commemorative
celebratory
boink.

Haiku VII

Cheeks pulled open wide,
I check your punctuation.
Hey there, asterisk!

~

Still-branched birds settle.
Prick-stuck, you yelp in surprise.
Restless wings take flight.

~

Post-coital cuddle:
fucked into silence that lasts
'til our bellies growl.

~

Her blue tank top dips.
She rides past, pedals flying.
Round, her ass recedes.

Fresh from the shower,
even here, it smells of soap.
I tongue. You tremble.

~

gator clamps grip tight
I shake the connecting chain
watch your titties dance

~

Polite, I tell her
that she puts on a fine spread —
ankle in each hand.

~

Tied to none but myself,
I point my toes at your touch.
The string tugs my balls.

Bonfire

Normally, I'd say you're no Penelope,
leaving me no path to Ithaca but breadcrumbs.
There's been no beacon kept lit on the shore,
    no horn or whistle or village bell,
    no neon roadside arrow sign,
    no borrowed map badly folded,
    no Waze shortcut through private land
    or Google Street View of unemptied city trash.

I am not greater than a fool's memory.
And there is no road I can see to take
back to a place I've never been.
A hero's wife might help. She might not.

Stand at the window and take off your top!
Let loose more than neighbors' whispers!
I can follow the swish of falling fabric.
I can imagine your breasts rise and descent.

Crumb by crumb, I will seek you.
Exposed and waiting, you'll be found.

At some point, we'll have waffles.

Vernal Fool

Not to argue with Tennyson,
but I saw a bare shoulder today.
It's spring all but certain,
and I have to say it isn't my fancy
what's doing antic turns.

A robin sings. A flower blooms.
I shed my winter furs for shirt sleeves
and walk out again — prick-ready, eager —
bounding to the greening table
where love's the whole menu once more.

New Year's Revelry

The ice in the champagne bucket
is practically alive. It kibbitzes as it melts,
rattles off suggestions as it settles, thinks itself
clever for proposing both nipple clamps
and fifty-year-old porn from Alpha France.
It knows us pretty well.

A second movie has the same actors as the first.
Dialogue washes over us without subtitles
as we attempt less-Continental midnight kisses
lit by the TV and one candle flame flickering
yellow on our unclothed skin, starting the year
with goosebumps and salted caramels.

Inspired to our feet, we're left to contemplate
the approximate height of an old Ottoman,
our own heights, what each inch might mean
if one kneels here, the other stands there,
the angles and the word for *protractor* in French,
the joy, the start, the finish, another year begun.

Fast Food, Precluded

We like to do it slow.
No late-night drive-thru,
Gas-N-Sip Mountain Dew,
fishnet stocking see-through,
cashier playing peek-a-boo,
doesn't matter who eats who
'cuz what you like is what we do,
five-course dinner made for two,
ain't no feast as good as you.
Slow, slow. Take it slow.
Nibble kibble. Crack and snack.
Savor. Flavor. Taste.
Lickety-lappedy-lunch.

The Hiss of Deflating Display Floaties

Last weekend of summer plus one,
the beach town yawns toward hibernation.
Seafood shacks shutter, still smelling of oil.

Ice cream stands and fudge shops,
the art galleries all finally close.
Locals reappear, blink, then vanish like moles.

We share a Hoodsie cup on a dune.
We drink hard cider from a jug.
We see three seals float by just offshore,

watching me finger you and you stroke me
on this our last beach day, no sunscreen used,
no need before winter's long, pale nights.

When is a plan not a plan? We stay 'til sunset.
We watch the day turn to night, watch the waves calm,
save our last condom for the drive-in's final show.

My Lover is Lush

My lover's kisses are a murmuration,
each single kiss too hidden among the many
to count as its own perfect bird.

Her breasts abound, so luxuriant
that each becomes itself a world
too large for a single hand to hold.

Her bush is verdant, fragrant —
a forest that lies just beyond the arc
of her softest belly curve.

Her cunt is a syrupy spring,
a golden well — a waterfall of sweets
too filling to fill, too deep to plumb.

My lover is opulent with her time
and lavish with her attentions.
She's everything virid, eternally ripe.

Snapshot

You and I are clueless observers,
never knowing a moment's passed
    until it already has, all echoes fading.
    Silence. Done.

This is how it happens.
This is how two ants,
    their mandibles raised to hug or hurt,
wind up stuck in the slipstream —
    their instant, now always,
    their always, never now.

This is how two ants become
caught in pine sap, picture taken,
    this amber moment,
    this La Brea timeout,
    this dinosaur footprint cast in plaster
        by a girl and her dad
        one Sunday morning in May.

None of those register forever —
no one thing maudlin or fragile,
    sentimental or saccharin,
    Hallmark, either channel or card.
Nothing begets nothing.

I knew you were the one
that time when you came
and laughed so hard
you pushed me out,
        still full mast, unspent,
        surprised by the cold
        and the sudden insistent squeeze.
It was the purest sound, the kindest hand.

We're frozen like Tater Tots,
        stored in a bag on a shelf
        next to Disney's head.

All of us are caught in that moment.
The amber. The laugh. The squeeze.

Bump in the Night

It's not like I expected your ghost
to show up in flowing sheets.
    A pair of overalls
    over a white T-shirt,
    crew socks and Docs
    seemed more likely from the start.
The dress is a good compromise.
It makes you look taller.
    Maybe you are taller.
    Maybe in this afterlife
    you get those extra two inches
    you always said made your sister lofty.
We stare at each other.
You're at the foot of the bed.
    I blink. Now you're at the side.
    No sounds, no footsteps.
    You float sideways as if
    this haunting's a dolly shot.
I decide to say it since you can't:
"I told you you fucked a penguin."
    A good punchline is a talisman.
    A good punchline is a contract.
    You smile and reach through the blankets
    to warm your hands between my legs.
You always wanted to go parking,
but we never went parking,
    never had sex in that red Malibu
    when we were both young, even younger
    than this young version of you,
    fading away, squeezing my cock ta-ta.

Within Reach

This is the nonchalance of the unknowing,
the chill disregard of a woman with eyes closed,
  seated in a small square room,
  on all sides surrounded by gloryholes
with proud stiff members projecting,
  bobbing inches from her face,
in theory within her grasp,
  untouched but knowable,
  unexplored but unrealized,
because why would there be such a room:
  a chair that rests in the middle,
  a red light that constantly hums,
  a ticking clock in purposeful dimness,
a woman calmly sitting, unaware of
silent cocks left dangling in warm, stirred air,
all waiting for just one eye to open,
the gasp of a single "Ah-ha!",
perhaps an open mouth,
perhaps a tempted hand.

Haiku VIII

We smooch good morning,
grateful there's one part of you
that rises early.

~

sweet new alfalfa
what she's mowed grows back slowly
I graze in stubble

~

Tied beneath the tree,
you wait for Santa knees up,
tinsel on your toes.

~

these winter evenings
so many layers of clothes
you're in there somewhere

paint orange their cocks
sway erect like daylilies
reaching for your sun

~

This — what you're holding —
tries to swell against your palm.
Pull him now to you.

~

fluffer his nutter
soon see such silly spasms
clean-up on Aisle 4

~

How whimpers carry
out her window into mine!
That's three and counting.

Dim Sum at Awesome House of Joy

Spinning, serene on a lazy Susan, a naked woman
lies centered on this our round table —
a lily and a teapot between her open legs,
curved spout erect, petals pink, shadows short,

her rotation without obfuscation, black hair
and powdered white skin, ass bisected,
all her flesh and folds, now in, now out of view.
The napkins are folded to resemble swans.

We are several drinks down before we're seated,
an all-male group with all the implications:
drunk and privileged, triumphant, project complete.
It's the business dinner I could not decline.

I eat. I drink tea. I answer when spoken to,
concentrating on avoiding missteps,
watching the clock, running out the clock,
begging the clock to throw me a bone.

I dine without hunger, interact with colleagues indulged,
toast and boast, blend in with the group as much or little
as one sesame seed on a bun coated in office drones.
Her feet move past. I glance up at calves.

Servers circle like sharks paid to ignore the chum,
bringing buns in baskets, steamed this, pan-fried that,
our tiny plates stacking up, a feast in fits and starts.
I dip Har Gao in chili sauce until her face comes again.

The table on a table moves, but she never does.
On her elbows, palms up, back arched, stoically staring
past our drunken faces at the walls, seeming to ignore
the talk of her looks, her body as parts, as dumplings,

seeming not to care which one might touch her,
fully resigned to how someone always does.
My boss, two levels up, pokes her foot with a chopstick.
She sees me seethe in silence before rotating away.

The dim sum slows until it stops, all plates removed.
Three women prepare her for dessert.
They place a dozen egg tarts beside her legs,
bowls of mango mousse near her arms.

They pile chunks of fruit on her back
until the juices run down her sides and ass
and pool near the flower, someone's idea of fun.
The diners wait, forks raised, chopsticks abandoned.

Her face spins 'round, and I catch her eye,
tipping my head in solidarity I haven't earned
as I stand, turn, walk toward the door without excuse.
Questions scatter on my back like rice and fall spent.

Just outside, the head waiter motions me near, presents
me with washcloths, her clothes, her pay in an envelope,
points me to a side door. "Stay. She will come to you."
I wait for her because someone should.

We all own the decadence of our coerced displays
and make guilty gifts of their observation.
We are subjugated by a lack of rent control,
and the necessity of buying our daily bread to eat.

A job is a job because we won't do it for free.
Around we go, spinning clockwise on a platter.
In such tiny bites, some eat as others spin,
all observers observed, tiny plates taken away.

Motion and Eventual Rest

We're marvelously amiss in afterglow,
    our covers covering nothing,
    our silent linens speaking volumes —
        the wrinkles, the spots of lube,
        the bottom sheet's top right corner
        pulled loose, its elastic no match
                for your fingers' coital clutch.

That the bed itself is still standing
is testament to retrofitted springs and added slats.

But the bed's new location —
    half a foot from the wall
    and beyond the reach of the morning alarm?
That's evidence of vector physics
        and your
            two turns
                on top.

About the Writer

In high school, S.A. Harper wrote poems in the style of Percy Bysshe Shelley — melodramatic, bleak, and strictly rhyming. Later, having failed deflowering in a graveyard during college, Harper forswore both iambic pentameter and lovers with lacy-cuffed shirts, gradually embracing free verse and non-sequiturs. Bunnies.

This is Harper's second poetry collection. Harper also writes erotic short stories. Those naturally have more words and fewer line breaks. However, body parts and their functions are incredibly similar in both mediums.

For other work by S.A. Harper,
please visit:

Word Oyster Press
wordoyster.com

You may contact the writer at:
saharper@wordoyster.com

www.ingramcontent.com/pod-product-compliance
Lightning Source LLC
LaVergne TN
LVHW050937080826
845145LV00004B/1303

* 9 7 8 0 9 9 7 7 0 8 4 4 8 *